Rounders

Produced in collaboration with the
National Rounders Association

Produced for A & C Black by

Monkey Puzzle Media Ltd
Gissings Farm, Fressingfield
Suffolk IP21 5SH

Published in 2006 by

A & C Black Publishers Ltd
38 Soho Square, London W1D 3HB
www.acblack.com

Third edition 2006

Copyright © 2006, 2001, 1994
National Rounders Association

ISBN-10: 0 7136 7897 6
ISBN-13: 978 0 7136 7897 0

A CIP record for this book is available from the
British Library.

Note: While every effort has been made to ensure
that the content of this book is as technically accurate
and as sound as possible, neither the author nor the
publisher can accept responsibility for any injury or
loss sustained as a result of the use of this material.

A & C Black uses paper produced with elemental
chlorine-free pulp, harvested from managed
sustainable forests.

Acknowledgements
Cover and inside design by James Winrow for
Monkey Puzzle Media Ltd.
Cover and all inside photographs courtesy of
the National Rounders Association.
Illustrations by Dave Saunders.

KNOW THE GAME is a registered trademark.

Printed and bound in China by C&C Offset Printing
Co. Ltd.

Note: Throughout the book players and officials are
referred to as 'he'. This should, of course, be taken
to mean 'he or she' where appropriate. Similarly, all
instructions are geared towards right-handed players
– left-handers should simply reverse these instructions.

CONTENTS

FOREWORD

On behalf of the National Rounders Association I am delighted that *Know the Game: Rounders* has proved to be a popular publication. It provides a sound base for the development of rounders skills and tactics, and an understanding of the rules.

Participation in rounders is increasing, as more children play at school and then continue to play in adult leagues that are spreading throughout the country.

The support of Sport England has enabled rounders to be developed in all areas, from coaching to officiating to participation at grass roots and international levels.

The standard and pace of the game continues to improve, and greater opportunities are becoming available for players of all ages and abilities to play this exciting, fast-moving sport. *Know the Game: Rounders* has played a major part in this, and we are delighted that this new, improved edition is now available.

Alison Howard
Director of Rounders
National Rounders Association

◀ Rounders is a fast-paced team game, which can be a lot of fun at all levels.

▶ The bat is a key piece of equipment in the game of rounders and players should learn to get the best out of it!

INTRODUCTION

Rounders is an exciting, fun sport of striking and fielding. Players develop fielding, batting, bowling and running skills.

THE GAME

- Rounders is a non-contact sport, so is suitable for mixed gender and mixed age teams. It is played by boys, girls, men and women.

- Rounders is played at varying levels of skill and competitiveness, from a game on the beach to an international-level match.

- Rounders can be adapted for players with disabilities.

- Rounders is played in 86% of all schools. There are over 40 adult leagues throughout England, with players aged 14 to the late 60s. In adult leagues the most common age range is 25–35.

- Rounders is an international sport, with England Rounders teams from age 13 to adult. It is also one of 31 sports selected to participate in the UK Coaching certificate.

THE GAME

Rounders is played between two teams. Ideally there are nine players on each side, though rounders can be played with as few as six players on either team. Each team bats in turn while the other fields. In a full game, each team has two innings.

BATTING AND SCORING

The object of the batting team is to hit the ball so that the batter is able to run round four posts and score a 'rounder'. If the batter hits the ball and reaches second post, a half-rounder is scored. Other scores are shown on page 14.

Batters can 'stay', or stop, at any post on the way round, reaching fourth post several balls later. They then have a chance to bat again, but do not score a rounder.

 The batter adjusts her position, ready to make contact with the ball.

BOWLING AND FIELDING

The bowler, backstop and fielders work together to get the batters out as quickly as possible, and to prevent them scoring rounders. Batters can be got 'out' if a fielder touches the next post they are heading for with the ball, or with the hand holding the ball. They are also out if a fielder catches a ball they have hit before it touches the ground. See pages 15, 26 and 27 for other ways in which a batter can be out.

The bowler stands in the bowling square. The backstop stands behind the batting square, but must not obstruct the hitting action of the batter. Most teams have one fielder on first post. The rest of the fielders are arranged by the team captain. The game can be very exciting if played by skilled players working together as a team.

INNINGS

A full game consists of two innings per team; the team with the greater number of rounders wins. An innings is over when there are no members of the batting team available to bat.

If one team is leading by five or more rounders after the first innings, the team with the lower score bats again. If the team with the lower first innings score cannot better its opponents' score in the second innings, the game is over and the higher-scoring team has won.

The player stretches to make the rounder before the fielder touches the post with the ball.

The official *Rules and Hints to Umpires* is available from the NRA Publications Secretary.

SUBSTITUTES

- Any or all of six substitutes, named before the start of the game, can join in at any dead-ball situation, such as if the bowler delivered a foul ball (after first informing the umpires and the other team).
- In a mixed team, a maximum of five males per team may be on the field of play at any one time.

EQUIPMENT

The equipment needed to play rounders is simple and inexpensive to buy. For safety reasons, all equipment should be of a manufacture approved by the NRA. Details of the NRA's equipment-safety policy can be obtained from the Equipment Secretary at the address given on page 56.

THE BAT

The bat can be of any length up to a maximum of 46cm. It should not be more than 17cm round the thickest part or weigh more than 370g. Approved bats are made of aluminium or wood.

> **Batters have to carry the bat with them around the track, so ideally each member of the batting team should have a bat.**

 Rules for contacting the post with the ball: **Left** – post touched by the fielder. **Centre** – if post and base are separated, base must be touched. **Right** – if base has moved from the marked spot, spot must be touched.

THE BALL

Rounders balls should be made of leather, weigh between 65g and 85g, and measure between 18cm and 20cm in circumference. The best quality balls are covered in white kid leather.

It is best to use cheaper balls for practice, and specially made, hard-wearing balls when playing on asphalt. They are all the same size and weight as the standard ball.

THE POSTS

Four posts are used, each 1.2m high, with a heavy base so that they are not knocked over easily or blown over by the wind. Bases should have no sharp projections or points, and the collar (where there is one) in which the post is fitted should be no higher than 50mm.

For the purposes of the rules, the post, not the base, is what should be touched with the ball by the fielder. However, if the post is somehow knocked away from the base, then the base should be touched. If the base is also moved from the marked spot, then the spot should be touched (see diagrams on page 8).

Posts driven into the ground are not permitted. The NRA recommends the use of approved rubber bases.

CLOTHING

Normal sports clothing and footwear is worn for rounders. If teams play in similar uniform, they can be identified by coloured bands, arm bands or playing bibs. During an official match, all players – substitutes included – must be clearly numbered.

> **Spiked footwear, including cricket boots, is not allowed in rounders. Studs are allowed providing they are no longer than 12mm.**

▶ Rounders balls are small and batters must develop the skill to hit them at speed.

THE PITCH

You can play rounders on any surface on which it is possible to run quickly (e.g. asphalt, all weather or grass), though mixed surfaces are not recommended.

AREA OF PITCH

The area needed for a rounders pitch is about the size of a soccer pitch (maximum 120m by 90m). A large area makes for a more open game, and both fielding and hitting improve. Even so, the game is still enjoyable played on a smaller area, even one surrounded by walls.

MARKED AREA

Avoid marking the pitch in the corner of the playing area as this restricts hitting. The forward/backward line should be parallel to the boundary fence.

Whatever the size of the playing area, certain distances must be standard. The essential measurements – the ones that must be the same on all pitches – are:

- The size of the bowling and batting squares, which the bowler and batter must stay within. These measurements are given on pages 12 and 13.

- The distance between batting and bowling squares, so that bowlers are always bowling the same distance, whatever pitch they are playing on.

- The distance between the batting square and the first post, because of the importance of the backstop's throw to first post.

Other distances can be less accurate without spoiling the game.

SETTING OUT THE PITCH

The simplest way of marking the positions of the posts relative to the batting square is by using lengths of string:

1. Put a peg into the ground where the right-hand front corner of the batting square is to be, and another peg at a distance of 17m at 90° to the front line of the batting square. This gives the position of second post.

2. Take a length of string measuring 24m and tie a knot in the centre (so each half will be 12m). Tie one end of the string to each peg and carry the centre knot out to the right until the string is taut. The knot gives the position of first post: mark it with a peg.

3. Carry the centre knot to the left. Pull the string taut. The knot gives the position of third post: mark it with a peg.

4. Take a length of string 17m long, with a centre knot so that each half is 8.5m. Tie one end to the peg at third post and the other to the peg first put in at the corner of the batting square. Carry the string to the left until it is taut. The knot gives the position of fourth post; mark it with a peg.

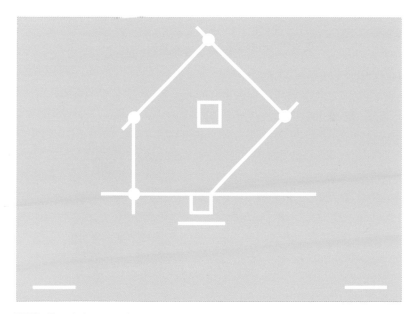

 The pitch: compulsory markings.

THE BOWLING SQUARE

Dimensions: 2.5m x 2.5m
To locate the centre of the front line of the square, stretch the 17m string from the first peg to the second post, then measure a distance of 7.5m along the string. The front line of the bowling square will then be 1.25m either side of the string and parallel to the front line of the batting square. The other three sides of the square can then be marked. It will be found that if the string is stretched between the first and third posts, it cuts the sidelines of the square 1m from the front line.

 The bowler delivers the ball with an underarm action.

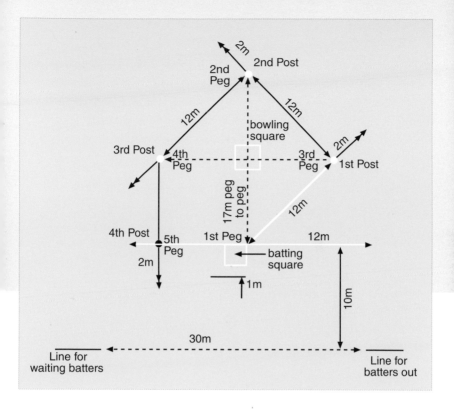

 The standard measurements of a rounders pitch.

THE BATTING SQUARE

Dimensions: 2m x 2m
The front line is made by marking a line extending 2m from the first peg, in a direct line towards fourth post and parallel to the front line of the bowling square. The remaining three sides of the square can then be marked. The front line of the square should be extended on each side. This will separate the backward and forward areas. A line should also be marked from the right-hand corner of the batting square to the first-post position.

At least 10m behind the backward/forward area line, and 15m either side of the front right-hand corner of the batting square, lines are drawn to mark the positions for waiting batters and batters who are out.

BASIC RULES

The rules of rounders have become more detailed as the game has developed. If you play in a competitive league or tournament you will probably play to the national rules. When you first play the game, more basic rules are fine – so long as everybody is playing to the same ones!

TEAMS

- Teams consist of a maximum of nine players and a minimum of six.
- Mixed teams should have a maximum of five males.

SCORING

There are several ways for teams to score a rounder or half-rounder.

- A rounder is scored if, after hitting the ball, the batter runs round the track and touches fourth post.
- A half-rounder is scored if, after hitting the ball, the batter reaches second post and is not out before another ball is bowled.
- A half-rounder is scored if, after missing the ball, the batter runs round the track and touches the fourth post.
- A half-rounder is scored if the fielder, in the opinion of the umpire, obstructs the batter.

- A half-rounder is awarded to the fielding team if a batter, while waiting to bat, obstructs a fielder.

Batters must touch fourth post as they run to or past it.

BOWLING

The bowler should deliver the ball:

- with a smooth and continuous underarm action
- with both feet within the bowling square before the ball is released
- within the reach of and to the hitting side of the batter
- below the top of the batter's head and above his or her knee
- so that it is not bowled directly at the batter
- so that it does not bounce before reaching the batting square.

If the bowler fails to comply with any of these rules, a 'no-ball' is called. See pages 24 and 25 for more information.

BATTER OUT

A batter is declared out if:

- the ball is caught after hitting the bat or the hand holding the bat (except on a no-ball)

- the batter's foot is over the front or back line of the batting square during the hitting action

- the batter runs inside a post (unless forced to do so by an obstructing fielder)

- a fielder touches a post to which a batter is running, with the ball or with the hand holding the ball

- the batter obstructs a fielder or intentionally deflects a ball being thrown by a fielder

- the batter overtakes another batter

- the batter loses contact with a post while waiting at it, if the bowler has possession of the ball in the bowling square

- the batter leaves a post at which he or she is waiting during the bowler's action, but before the ball is released

- the batter deliberately drops or throws the bat.

▼ 'Stumped out' is the term used when the fielder 'stumps' or 'tags' the post and the batter is out.

STARTING THE GAME

The captains toss a coin, and the winner decides either to field or to bat. The fielding team then takes its positions on the pitch, while the batting team waits in turn for a chance to bat.

FIELDING POSITIONS

The bowler, a backstop and a first-post fielder take standard positions. The other players go to their natural fielding positions – where they themselves hit and therefore where they expect their opponents to hit. Standard positions are shown in the diagram below.

Key to diagrams

B – bowler	4P – fourth post
BS – backstop	1D – first deep
1P – first post	2D – second deep
2P – second post	3D – third deep
3P – third post	and so on

CHANGING THE FIELD

The captain will usually change the fielding positions of the team once he or she has had a chance to judge the capabilities of the batters:

- if there are big hitters, more fielders may be needed further out in the field
- for weaker or more nervous hitters, the fielders could come closer in
- the fielding positions may also need to change if a left-hander is batting.

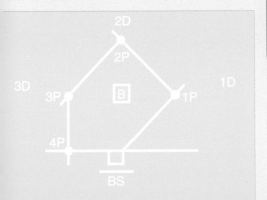

Standard fielding positions: arrange the field to suit the ability of the players.

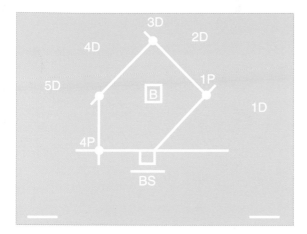

In this formation, there are five deep fielders. Backstop is available to cover fourth post.

THE BATTING SIDE

The batting side has to wait in the backward area behind the marked lines. If a waiting player moves from these lines and impedes a fielder, a half-rounder is awarded to the fielding team. The batting side should use the waiting time to study the bowling and the placing of the fielders, and to judge the other team's capabilities. Working out where the weaker fielders are placed will give experienced batters a chance to place the ball in that area when they hit it.

Whether you are batting, bowling or fielding, keep your eyes on the ball at all times.

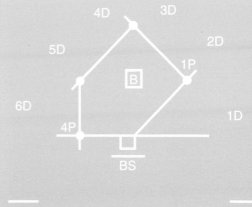

Here, there are six deep fielders. The bowler could take fourth post with backstop covering; or the backstop could take fourth with the first post fielder covering.

17

BATTING TECHNIQUE

Batters can stand where they like in the square, so long as their feet do not cross the front or back line while they are hitting or trying to hit the ball. Before hitting the ball study the position of the fielding team: hit the ball into the least protected area of the field.

Ensure the tip of the bat is raised higher than your wrist when contacting the ball.

HOW TO HIT

'Hitting' the ball means striking it with the bat, or with the hand holding the bat.

1. Stand sideways to the bowler when receiving the ball (for right-handed players, left shoulder forwards and weight on the left foot).

2. Hold the bat so that the tip is above the level of the wrist. Watch the ball from the bowler's hand all the way to the bat.

Some players hold the bat in front of them, letting the weight of the bat be taken by the other hand. Others find it helpful to prepare for the hit by holding the bat behind them in the back-lift position. At the right moment the bat is swung forward to meet the ball.

> **Batters do not have to stand still in the square; the space is theirs to use.**

In batting there are four important points to master.

1. Arm movement
Swing back from the shoulder, with the elbow lifted away from the body; stay relaxed. Hit the ball by quickly straightening the elbow with a strong swift flick and a turn of the hand, so that the knuckles are facing the ground. This turn of the wrist and arm adds speed to the hit and direction to the ball.

2. Footwork
As the ball approaches, you have a split second to decide how to move your feet in order to make the hit. If you are right-handed and hold the bat lifted, your weight will be on the right foot. As you swing the bat forwards your weight transfers to the left foot.

If the bat is held out in front, the weight is swung on to the right foot as the bat is raised backwards, then forwards on to the left foot as the hit is made – this will give more power to the stroke.

3. Turning the shoulders
Turning the back shoulder forwards as the hit is made adds force to the stroke.

4. Timing
Blend arm, foot and shoulder movements into one continuous action. Practice will help you lift your arm just before the ball reaches you, so that you can swing forwards to hit as you shift your weight and turn your shoulders.

A long hit over the head of the first-post fielder is further from fourth post, making it harder for the fielders to get you out.

Transferring your weight on to your front foot when contacting the ball with give the hit more force.

PLAYING THE GAME

The essence of rounders is that the batting team is trying to score. The fielding team is trying to stop this, whilst trying to get the batters out so that they have a chance to bat themselves.

SCORING A ROUNDER

Each batter is entitled to one 'good' ball. Having hit or attempted to hit it, batters must leave the batting square and run round the track. If they reach and touch fourth post before the next ball is bowled, they score one rounder if they hit the ball, or a half-rounder if they missed it.

The batter may 'stay', or stop, at any post on the way round. Batters are safe at a post as long as they keep contact with the post by touching it with a hand or bat. As soon as further balls are bowled, the batter can run on to the next post or further, but does not score when reaching the fourth post. The only advantage to getting round in this way is that you are not out, so you can bat again.

The batter remains in the backward area until it is his or her turn to bat again. When batters are out, the sequence of the batting order remains unchanged.

The batter must run outside the post, otherwise they will be out.

POINTS TO REMEMBER

When a fielder touches a post with the ball it affects the game in the following ways:

- A batter who is moving towards a post from the previous post is out.
- It prevents a 'live' batter (one to whom the current ball was bowled) from scoring if he or she is stopped at the previous post. For instance: if the 'live' batter has reached first post, second post should be touched to stop the batter from scoring. If the batter has reached second post, third post should be touched; if the batter has reached third post, fourth post should be touched.

A fielder touching a post has no other effect on the game, and does not prevent any batter from running right round the track, including running to posts which have been touched by a fielder.

BALL IN PLAY

The ball is in play from the time it leaves the bowler's hand until he or she again has possession of the ball and is in the square. A batter can continue to run round the track until the bowler has the ball and is in the bowling square. There is no other way of stopping a batter from running, but the batter must be careful not to be stumped out at a post.

 The fielder stumps the post by touching it with the ball.

21

BATTERS STOPPING AT A POST

On the way round the track, the batter may stop at a post if the fielding is better than expected and it seems dangerous to go on. If the fielders misjudge a throw, the batter can run on again. (Only when the ball and bowler are back in the bowling square does play have to stop.) If the batter succeeds in reaching fourth post, a rounder is scored.

For example, a batter hits a ball deep into the field and runs. The batter reaches second post and makes contact with the post. It looks impossible to get to fourth post. The deep fielder overthrows the ball – it was meant for the bowler, but it pitches just outside first post. The batter sees it is safe to run on, and arrives at fourth post, scoring a rounder.

TIPS FOR BATTERS

- A batter should always run as far as possible, to clear the way for the next batter, who may be a good runner.
- There can never be two batters at one post. For example, a batter is at second post and is caught up by the next batter. The umpire instructs the first batter to run on. They may then be put out at the next post. If the second batter overtakes they are out.
- Batters are out if they run inside a post.

The batter must maintain contact with the post at all times as they wait to run on, otherwise the fielder could stump them out.

FIELDER TOUCHING POST

If a batter stops at a post and a fielder touches the post immediately ahead, the batter can subsequently run on, but cannot score. For example, a batter has reached third post. A fielder touches fourth post and then throws the ball carelessly back to the bowler, who misses it. Nobody is backing up so the ball trickles away between second and first posts. The batter gets home with ease, but because the post immediately ahead was touched, there is no score. The umpire calls 'No score'.

Imagine a match where everyone has frozen in the places shown in the diagram. The stumped fourth post puts out batter A. It does not stop the other batters from getting home safely later, nor does it prevent batter D from scoring on this ball.

Stumping second post would prevent batter D from scoring, but again would not prevent any batter running to fourth post on this ball later in the throw.

▼ Batter D is the 'live' batter. Touching fourth puts out A but does not prevent D from scoring.

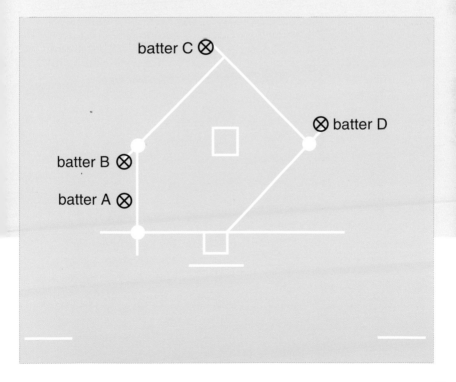

batter C ⊗

⊗ batter D

batter B ⊗

batter A ⊗

BATTERS KEEPING CONTACT WITH A POST

When batters are at a post they should either hold it with their hand or keep contact with their bat. If they lose contact, they can be put out by a fielder touching the next post with the ball in hand.

Batters in contact with the post can move on as soon as the next ball leaves the bowler's hand.

If a batter overruns a post, he or she can come back and make contact with that post, providing they have run straight on and not changed direction. To stay in, the batter must have touched the post while running past it before the fielder.

OBSTRUCTION BY A BATTER

Batters should run from post to post in a direct line. They have right of way and are in no danger of obstructing a fielder. If batters run off a direct course and collide with a fielder, and this prevents the fielder from fielding, the batter will have caused an 'obstruction'. The batter is given 'out' by the umpire. Any rounder scored due to that obstruction is discounted.

Batters are also out if they deliberately kick or touch the ball as they run round the track. The running track extends 2m beyond fourth post.

NO-BALLS

The ball must be bowled so that it would reach the batter within the limits shown in the diagram top left on page 25. (This imaginary rectangle changes according to the size and reach of each batter.) Otherwise the umpire calls 'no-ball' and batters need not run (though they can, and then may score in the usual way). Batters cannot be caught out or touched out at first post from a no-ball.

BACKWARD HITS

If the batter mistimes his or her shoulder turn or moves their feet too soon, the ball may drop into the backward area. If this happens, batters can only run to first post. They can, however, run on the moment the ball crosses the forward/backward line, for example when a fielder throws it back across the line.

> The best way for a right-handed batter to keep in contact with the post is to change the bat to their left hand as they run.

GOOD BALLS INTO BAD

Umpires will not call 'no-ball' if the batter turns good balls into no-balls by walking into them or by stepping away to make them wide. Some players, finding hitting difficult, unconsciously make one of these mistakes.

If you find no-balls that are too high or too low are easy to hit, go all out for them – you cannot be caught out.

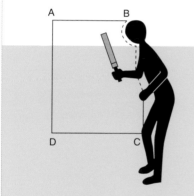

AB – level with the top of the batter's head.
CD – level with the batter's knees.
AD – the limit of the batter's reach.
BC – a line by the side of the batter's body (balls close to the body and difficult to hit are not no-balls).

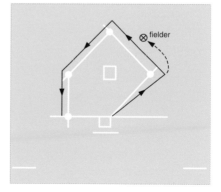

If a batter runs off course (dotted line) and obstructs a fielder he is out.

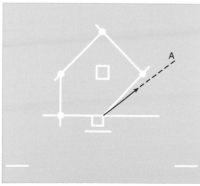

If a batter is running so quickly that he overruns the post (A), he can return to the post. If he runs on in the direction of the next post, he may not return.

BATTER OUT

Batters are out if:

- the ball is caught after hitting the bat or the hand holding the bat (except on a no-ball)
- their foot projects over the front or back line of the batting square before they hit the ball or it has passed them

- they run inside a post, unless prevented from reaching it by an obstructing fielder
- a fielder touches the post immediately ahead with the ball or the hand holding the ball, while the batter is running to that post and before the batter has touched it (except first post in the case of a no-ball)

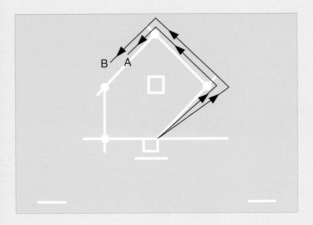

The diagram shows batter B overtaking A. Batter B is out.

Here, batter A is out for running inside the post.

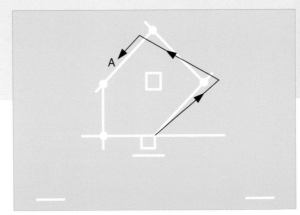

- they obstruct or verbally mislead a fielder, or intentionally deflect the course of the ball

- they overtake another batter

- they lose contact with a post or run at any time when the bowler has the ball and is in the bowling square (except on an overrun or unless ordered to do so by an umpire)

- they lose contact with a post or run during the bowler's action before the ball is released

- after having been ordered to make contact with a post they have not done so

- they deliberately drop or throw their bat.

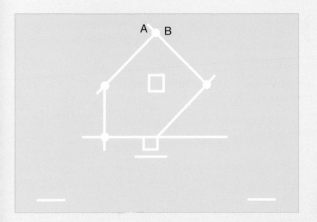

Two batters at a post. Batter A has to run on. If the next post is touched while he is running to it, he is out.

If second post is touched before Batter A arrives, A is out. Batter B can stay at the post, and is not out.

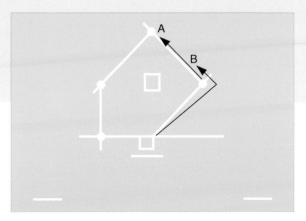

SIDE OUT

Rounders is unusual in that in the right circumstances, the whole team can be put out in one go. If there is no batter waiting a turn to bat, all the batters on the running track can be put out simultaneously by the ball being thrown full pitch (without bouncing) or touched into the batting square by any fielder, as long as none of the batters have reached and touched fourth post.

If there is no batter waiting a turn to bat, and the bowler has possession of the ball in the bowling square, the innings is declared over.

▼ The last batter in continues to try and score rounders until he or she is put out in the usual way.

SCORING SIDE OUT

When there are no players waiting to bat, and the fielders have stumped the batting square, all the players are out and no score is made e.g. the batter gets to second/third base but is out so does not score. If the ball is returned to the bowler in the bowling square then the innings is over but any score is recorded e.g. the batter gets to second/third base and scores a half rounder.

 Side out: the ball is thrown full pitch into the batting square.

Side out: the ball is touched into the square.

LAST BATTER IN

If only one batter is left, he or she is given the chance to hit at three 'good' balls. The batter need not run when the first two 'good' balls are bowled, but when the third 'good' ball comes, the batter must run. The fielding side tries to put the batter out in the normal way or place. As usual, touching fourth post has no effect unless the batter has passed third post.

If the batter fails to hit all three balls, the backstop puts the batter out by placing the ball in the batting square and the innings is closed.

The last batter can score from no-balls. The last batter cannot be caught out off a no-ball, but when running can be put out in the normal way. If the last batter scores a rounder, he or she is entitled to a rest of one minute, and then has the chance to hit three more 'good' balls and so on.

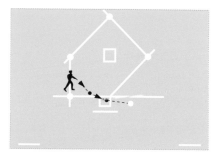

Not out: if the ball pitches outside the square and then travels into the square, the side is not out.

▶ Rounders players need to use speed and agility if they are to be first to the post!

BOWLING TECHNIQUE

The bowling action in rounders is based entirely on underarm throwing. The simplest method for a beginner to practise is an underarm throw aimed at the backstop's hands.

BOWLING ACTION

If you are right-handed, stand sideways to the backstop with your left foot forwards. Have your weight on the right foot, changing to the left foot as your arm swings forward. As the ball leaves your hand, turn your shoulders with a strong follow-through towards the batter.

The ball must be bowled in the direction of the batting square. If a batter lets go of a post because of a dummy ball, they are to be allowed to return to their original position.

> When learning to bowl, try to visualise the rectangular space into which your ball must go.

The bowling action should be smooth.

NO-BALLS

A no-ball will be called if:

- the ball reaches the batter outside the limits of the imaginary rectangle (see page 25)
- the ball fails to reach the batter
- the bowler steps out of the bowling square during the bowling action, i.e. before releasing the ball
- the ball bounces before reaching the batter.

FOOTWORK

When the simple bowling action has been learnt, bowlers will find that they can make the ball travel faster if they step forward as they bowl. To do this (for right-handers):

1. Stand at the back of the bowling square with your left side towards the batter. Hold the ball in your right hand and point your left arm in the direction in which you are bowling.

2. Step sideways with your left foot, lift your right arm behind you and close your right foot up to the left.

3. Step forwards with your left foot, bend your left knee, turn your shoulders and bowl.

While swinging the right arm forwards, balance the body by simultaneously swinging the left arm backwards. This action should be smooth and rhythmical.

 Step forwards to bowl with more force, using your free arm to balance.

ADVANCED BOWLING SUGGESTIONS

From the simple bowling action other ideas can be practised.

Speed

- The length of the bowling square (2.5m) allows for a run up before the ball is released. The bowler can step out of the square once the ball has been released. This allows for bowlers to increase their momentum and therefore the speed at which the ball can be delivered.

- Learn to change the speed of delivery even if you are using the same bowling action.

Spin and swing

- Change your grip so that you can turn your fingers as the ball is released, to make the ball spin.

- Change your grip and the swing of your arm, then the ball will swing either away from or into the batter.

 The bowler can step out of the square once the ball is released.

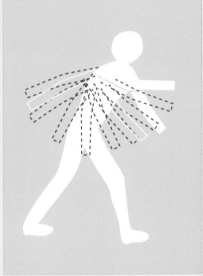

Use the same action but change the delivery to deceive the batter.

Bowling hint: keep your eyes on the backstop's hands and follow through.

Direction

- Change the angle of your run across the square and the ball will arrive at the batter from a different direction.

- Lower the position of your hand on delivery and the ball will rise up at the batter.

- A 'donkey-drop' – a high ball which arrives at the batter at the correct height – falls down towards the batter.

Different hands

If the bowler can bowl equally well with either hand, this may confuse the batter.

Bend the knees in the running stride, and release the ball lower than normal so that it rises up to the batter – making it harder to hit.

The 'donkey drop': a high ball that reaches the batter at the correct height.

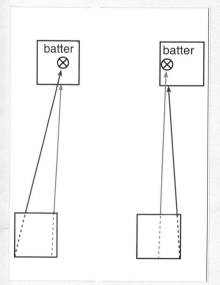

Change of direction: blue line – bowler runs straight across the square; red line – bowler runs diagonally across the square.

All bowling variations should be delivered with a smooth and continuous underarm action, and produce a 'good' ball as defined by the rules.

FIELDING SKILLS AND TACTICS

Fielding is a team activity. The object is to keep the batting team's scoring to a minimum. Every fielder must be alert throughout the innings. Fielders should be ready to move, not rooted to the spot. They must keep their eye on the ball, and be ready to backup and cover other fielders.

SIMPLE FIELD SETTINGS

In a game for beginners, the fielders are arranged in two semi-circles. The inner semi-circle contains the four post fielders and the backstop. The outer semi-circle consists of three deep fielders, who cover the post fielders and field long hits. The ninth player is the bowler.

Field placings can change during an innings. Fielders should watch for directions from the backstop, who can see the whole field. The field is changed for strong or weak batters, and left-handers.

ADVANCED FIELD SETTINGS

The best teams operate more complicated fielding systems. The inner semi-circle comprises the bowler, backstop and first-post fielder, who also covers second post. The backstop also covers fourth post. The outer semi-circle contains the other six fielders in an arc. All the fielders are ready to cover each other.

 Fielding skills: player moving to give cover to other fielder.

FIELDING TIPS

- Few hits go to the area behind first post, but when they do they can be winning ones. The first deep fielder has to stay alert.

- Have a plan of action for when a batter hits the ball. Each fielder should know what to do and where to throw the ball. The backstop will call the instructions. This saves thinking time, and makes fielding smoother and more efficient.

- Beware of obstructing a running batter, especially near the posts. The first-post fielder should be careful when receiving bad throws from the backstop; these could force an obstruction. Instead, the first-post fielder can catch the ball and allow the batter to reach the post, or leave the ball for the first deep fielder to field. The ball can then be returned to the bowler.

- Accurate throws to the bowler and other fielders are crucial.

- Remember, more than one batter can be put out at a time. Fielders should be aware of all the opportunities.

STOPPING A ROUNDER

If a batter makes a hit, a fielder touching the post ahead of the post the batter has reached prevents the rounder from being scored. So does returning the ball to the bowler in the bowling square before the 'live' batter reaches the third post.

Fielders should remain alert with their eyes on the ball at all times.

CATCHING

It is important to get into the correct position for catching. More catches are missed by failure to do this than by failure of the hands to close on the ball.

The ideal catching technique can be summarised as follows:

- Move quickly to get in line with the flight of the ball.
- Keep the body balanced and watch the ball closely.
- Aim to catch the ball level with your face.
- Spread your fingers so that the ball is caught in them.
- Your hands should 'give' to the force of the ball. This 'give' is generally in the direction the ball is already travelling, though sometimes a ball can be snatched out of its path. Fast-travelling balls need more give than slow ones.

CATCHING TIPS

When the ball is hit, judge if possible where it is going to land. If a ball is going over your head, move back quickly, keeping your weight forwards. If it is a very long hit, turn round and run hard so that you can at least field it on its first bounce, even if you can't catch it.

Short quick steps are best if a fielder has to move to the left or right to get behind wide balls. Two hands are always safer than one for catching, but right- and left-hand catching should be practised.

 Maintain your balance underneath the direction of the ball.

FIELDING BALLS ON THE GROUND

A ball travelling along the ground must be gathered as quickly as possible. Practise fielding this kind of ball approaching from both the right and the left.

Stand with your weight distributed equally on both feet. As the ball is hit, put the weight on the balls of your feet, slightly bend your knees, keep your arms and hands ready, and start moving into the line of the ball.

Try to anticipate the ball's line of flight. If it is moving slowly, run to meet it. If it is moving quickly, run to get behind it. Fielders should always be able to see their hands as they pick up the ball. Keep your wrists forwards and your hands round the ball. The ball should be moved quickly into the throwing hand and returned, so that the fielding is speeded up.

When stopping the ball, fielders should get right behind it and watch it into their hands. Most fields are uneven, so the ball can bounce awkwardly and unexpectedly.

 Keep watching the ball until you have safely caught it.

OVERARM THROWING

The ball is thrown above or about the level of the shoulders. This throw is used for long distances and needs plenty of practice to make sure of accuracy.

Action

- Stand sideways to the player to whom you are throwing, with the weight on your back foot (i.e. the right foot if the ball is held in the right hand).

- Bend your throwing arm slightly and hold it well away from your body. Drop the shoulder of your throwing arm and raise the other arm to give balance. Now bring the front shoulder and arm into the line of the direction of the throw.

- Make the throw with a strong forward turn of the shoulders, bringing the hand with the ball forwards by extending the elbow and flexing the wrist. Complete the throw by transferring the weight on to the front foot and bringing your throwing shoulder into the lead. This simultaneous change of weight and twist of the shoulders gives ease of movement and adds length to the throw. A strong wrist flick helps the flight of the ball.

ACCURATE THROWS

Aim to throw the ball directly into the hands of the receiver, for three reasons:

1. A bounced ball is often difficult to stop because the surface of the ground is seldom flat.

2. As the post area is small and crowded with players, post fielders may have difficulty in fielding a ball unless it falls directly into their hands. There is also a danger that a fielder may obstruct a batter by moving towards an inaccurate throw.

3. A direct throw is quicker and surer: the receiving fielder may have to use the ball immediately to touch a post, or to put it in the square to end an innings.

UNDERARM THROWING

This throw is most useful for short distances. The ball is thrown from below the level of the shoulders and is similar to the bowling action.

Action

- Hold the ball in your throwing hand and swing your arm backwards, close to your body. Right-handed players step forwards with the left foot and at the same time swing the right arm forwards and release the ball.

- When the ball has been released, your fingers should be pointing in the direction of the throw, at the receiver's hands.

Ensuring your throw is directed to a post fielder can save vital seconds when stumping the post.

- If the ball goes too high, it has been released too late and your fingers will be pointing above the target area. If it is too low, the ball has left your hand too soon and your fingers will be pointing below the target area.

When the basic underarm throw has been mastered, you can make a more powerful throw by adding a flick of your wrist as you release the ball.

INDIVIDUAL FIELDING POSITIONS

Where you play will define the specific skills you need to practise. It is very important that you acquire these skills as they key into the game and the other players will rely upon you.

BOWLER

The bowler's greatest value is that when he or she has the ball in the bowling square, no batter may pass or leave a post. Remember, the bowler remains an important member of the fielding team even after the ball has been bowled.

For example, teams that field with an outside semi-circle of six fielders sometimes use the bowler to receive a poor throw from the first deep fielder after a hit in that direction.

A batter hits the ball and runs to second post. The ball is returned to the bowler. If the batter waiting at third post loses contact with the post, a throw to fourth would result in the batter being put out. On the other hand, a bad throw to fourth post or a careless return to the bowler might result in the batter at second post getting home and scoring a full rounder. Perhaps it is wiser for the bowler always to keep the ball unless the batter who hit it has been put out or prevented from scoring.

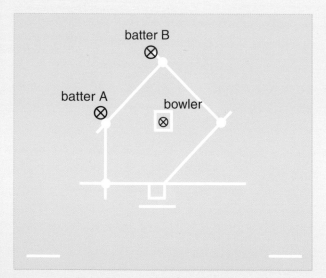

Batter B is the 'live' batter, but he cannot run on and score a rounder if the bowler has possession of the ball in the bowling square.

BACKSTOP

The backstop needs to be agile and full of stamina, and an accurate thrower. The ball must always be thrown on the inside of the posts; otherwise, the fielder may be forced to obstruct the batter.

Backstops should practise standing as close to the batter as possible (but always behind the backstop line and without impeding the batter's hitting action), in order to catch the ball before it bounces. The backstop should move according to the bowler's action and should practise with all the team's bowlers to get used to their different actions.

The backstop nearly always throws to first post, but this is not essential. If the batter in the square is weak and there is a good batter running to third post, a throw to third might be better. Backstops sometimes drop a ball instead of catching it because they are anxious about throwing the ball to get a batter out at a post. The way to avoid this is to concentrate on the catch before you even think about the throw.

Backstop should watch the ball not the batter.

If you are bowling, do not bowl until all of your fielders are in position, ready to field the ball.

TIPS FOR BACKSTOPS

Backstops should:

- stand ready to move quickly
- field behind the bat, not behind the batter
- always be careful not to be unsighted by the batter.

41

POST PLAY

Post fielders, like all other fielders, should stand ready with their weight evenly balanced and feet slightly apart, ready to move quickly in any direction. Stay on the inside and close to the post, so that you can touch it quickly without turning.

- If a team has a player at each of the posts in an inner semi-circle (as in most junior games), low balls and short catches are picked up by these post fielders.

- If the 'live' batter stops at a post and a fielder touches the post immediately ahead of the batter, the batter cannot then score even if he or she subsequently runs on.

- It is possible, with quick teamwork, to catch out one batter, touch out a second, and throw the ball to another post fielder to touch out a third.

 First post stands inside the track and focuses on the backstop.

FIRST-POST FIELDER

All teams field with a first-post fielder, except in special circumstances as described above, as the batter is often put out at first post after missing the ball.

Although it is not compulsory to have fielders standing by the other posts, some teams like to arrange their fielders in this way.

First-post fielders need good 'give' in their catching action, as balls are often thrown swiftly from the backstop. Left-handed players make good first-post fielders: their left hand is near the post and they are able to touch it without turning.

- First-post fielders should practise accurate throwing to third and fourth posts, making it possible to get out a second batter with the same ball.

- The first-post fielder should back-up the bowler when balls come from the deep field beyond third and fourth posts.

- First-post should also back-up in the batting square if there is likely to be a put out in the square at the end of an innings and the backstop is backing up at fourth post.

- When a left-handed player is batting, the first-post fielder must be ready to field oblique hits on the right of the batting square, including mishits into the backward area.

The first-post fielder normally goes into the deep field for the last batter. He or she is no longer needed at the first post as the ball may be put out in the batting square.

 Players waiting at first post.

A batter can only be put out at a post if he or she is moving towards it when it is touched with the ball or the hand holding the ball.

SECOND-POST FIELDER

The second-post fielder is also partly a deep fielder, and should be able to cover a wide area and make long throws. The bowler takes the second-post fielder's place in emergencies, for example when the fielder has had to run to collect a ball. Second-post fielders often have to work 'blind', as the bowler's action can obstruct their view of the batter.

THIRD-POST FIELDER

The third-post fielder should be an experienced player: this is probably the most important post position. Third post frequently receives catches and many low-driven ground balls. The fielder must take care not to obstruct running batters when a ball is driven wide of the post, or when taking inaccurate throws from deep field or from first post.

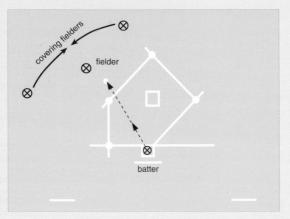

Fielders should always be ready to cover for each other.

A covering fielder positions himself behind fourth-post fielder, enabling himself to pick-up the throw if it goes astray.

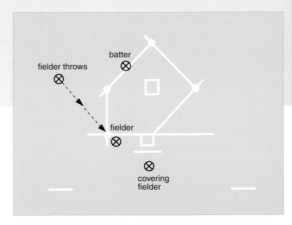

FOURTH-POST FIELDER

The fourth-post fielder needs safe hands for widely differing types of ball:

- long throws from deep field
- short hits and catches from the batter
- quick passes from third post
- frequent throws from first post, to put out a second batter after one has been put out at first post.

DEEP FIELDERS

Deep fielders must be swift, and able to catch any kind of ball and anticipate the direction of the ground balls. They should be ready to cover each other. The first deep fielder should also be ready to cover first post for bad throws from the backstop.

- Deep fielders should listen for calls from the fielders in the inner circle (usually the backstop), so that they know where to throw the ball.
- Long and accurate throwing is a skill that needs to be practised.
- Throw the ball so that the fielders on the posts do not obstruct the batter running round the track.

 All eyes are on the ball as the 'live' batter prepares to make a hit.

A GOOD TEAM

In matches between two teams equally good at bowling, batting and fielding, one side can be far more successful. Why? What makes a good team? They play as a team, not nine individuals. They work together and help each other throughout the game.

A good team discuss tactics before taking to the field.

TACTICS

Everyone in a team needs to know the rules, which will help them play the game intelligently. For example, if they bat first and make a low score, they will probably set a defensive field. This is a field chosen for a specific set of circumstances: it will be important to prevent the opposing team from scoring, as well as to get them out. The bowler will be extra careful to avoid offering balls that can be hit easily into the vulnerable area behind the first post, perhaps by bowling mainly from the right-hand side of the square, diagonally across the batter.

Another example of team tactics; when only two batters remain, with one stronger than the other, the team may decide to avoid putting out the weaker of the pair. If the weaker batter can only reach first post when he or she bats, there is a good chance of putting both batters out on the next ball, by placing the ball in the batting square. The more dangerous batter is thus prevented from receiving 'the best of three'.

When batting, the players need to get as far round the track as possible, moving on at every opportunity until the bowler has the ball. If there is an overthrow or misfield, it is far better to be already at third post than to be waiting at second. They will turn fielding lapses into rounders by putting pressure on the post fielders.

THE BEST RESULT

Good teams are usually filled with players who enjoy the game but take it seriously. They probably will not always win every game, but are trying to get the best possible result given their abilities, by making the most of the opportunities arising during the game.

All rounders teams bat, bowl and field. Make sure your team is one that bats, bowls, fields and THINKS.

 Team-mates should be able to communicate well in order to get the best out of their performance.

THE CAPTAIN

Captains should take responsibility for the whole team. They need to know the rules of rounders inside out.

A CAPTAIN'S DUTIES

A captain's duties include the following:

- Tossing a coin for choice of innings.
- Deciding the batting order and, if necessary, changing it for the second innings. (The umpires must be notified when any change is made.)

A good captain, often the backstop, who knows his players' skills inside out can determine the outcome of a match.

- If there are scorers, the captain must see that they have the batting order and are notified of any changes for the second innings.
- If the team uses arm bands or numbers, the captain should make sure they are worn.
- Arranging the field (in consultation with the bowlers).
- Changing the bowlers correctly. The procedure for this is: when the ball is in the bowler's hands in the square, the captain signals to the umpires for a pause, changes the bowler, then lets the umpires know the changes are finished.
- Examining the pitch before a match begins. Apart from clear and correct measurements, there should be a solid line defining the forward and backward area.
- Making substitutions, if required, in a dead-ball situation. The two umpires and the other team must be informed of this change.
- Thanking the umpires and scorers at the end of the match.

A captain must also be able to motivate their players if they are not making rounders.

It is wise to make the backstop the captain, as they can see the whole field in front of them and can make the best decisions.

UMPIRES

Players who are keen to understand the game should try umpiring. There are two umpires, the batters' umpire and the bowler's umpire.

Though the umpires' duties are divided, they must both concentrate on the game at all times and consult each other over difficult points. That way, if one umpire is unsighted, the other can help him or her make a decision.

Both umpires must watch to see that batters do not start to run during the bowler's action, before the ball is released. For infringements of this rule by the batting side, the umpire declares the offender(s) out.

 The bowler's umpire watches second post and the action at third.

SCORING

The simplest way of keeping score is for both umpires to have a piece of paper and a pencil. On this they keep a tally of rounders and half-rounders as they are scored, and a record of the number of players out. The umpire also calls the total score after each score.

> Umpiring decisions should be called loudly, so that they can be heard by all players.

BATTERS' UMPIRE

The batters' umpire stands where it is possible to see the batter and the first post, without having to turn his or her head. This means as far back as possible, remembering that the umpire also has to be able to see the front lines of both squares. Badly marked squares or unmown grass areas will force the umpire to stand nearer than is comfortable.

- The batters' umpire watches the ball as it passes the batter, and calls 'No-ball!' if it is above or below the limits described on page 25.

- Donkey-drops must be watched carefully. When they are travelling between the bowler and the batter they may be any height, but they must pass the batter at the correct height, otherwise, they are no-balls. 'No-ball!' must be called loudly enough for all players to hear. Remember: the height of the ball is judged in relation to the batter's height.

- The batters' umpire must also watch the play at first and fourth posts. If either of these posts is touched as a batter is running towards it, the umpire must call 'Out!'

- The batters' umpire must watch for catches and call 'Out!' if the ball is held. No part of the ball must touch the ground. The umpire must watch in case the ball is thrown on to another fielder to try to put out a second batter with the same ball.

- The batters' umpire must call 'Rounder!' when a batter touches fourth post, having completed the circuit before the next ball is bowled. The umpire calls 'No score!' if a batter completes a circuit having run on after a 'live' post has been touched by a fielder.

▼ The batter's umpire moves from position to gain a better view of proceedings.

BATTERS' UMPIRE (CONTINUED)

- If the ball drops into the backward area, the umpire's call is 'Backward hit!'.

- The batters' umpire must watch the front line of the bowling square in case the bowler steps over it before the ball has been released. Bowlers are allowed to step out after the ball has left their hand.

- The batters' umpire watches the bowler's wrist action. The bowler is not allowed to jerk the ball, but must deliver it smoothly.

- The batters' umpire must watch the front and back lines of the batting square. If the batter steps over these lines in hitting the ball, he or she is out.

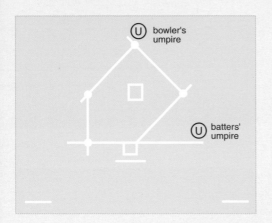

Suggested positions of umpires. If only one umpire is available, he should adjudicate from the bowler's umpire position.

Umpires work as a team. Be ready to move to a better position. Consult but do not publicly overrule each other's decision.

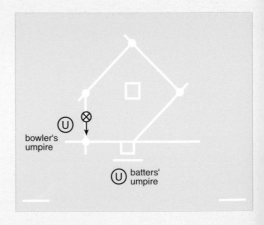

UMPIRING OBSTRUCTION

If a batter, when off course, obstructs a fielder, he or she is given out. If a fielder obstructs, the batter is awarded a half-rounder.

Obstruction may occur:

a) When a deep fielder runs into the post area to take a catch between the posts.
b) When a post fielder tries to put out a batter and gets in the way.

BOWLER'S UMPIRE

- The bowler's umpire calls 'Play!' to begin the game. If a team is slow to begin again after a no-ball has been bowled, or when there is a bowling change, the umpire calls 'Play!' again.

- The bowler's umpire calls 'No-ball!' if the ball passes the batter on either side of the imaginary rectangle shown on page 25. The ball may swerve in and out, so a no-ball should not be called before the ball reaches the batter. The no-ball is the batter's fault if he or she moves into or draws away from the line of the ball.

- The bowler's umpire gives decisions at second and third posts for in/out, obstructions, or when a batter runs inside the posts.

- The bowler's umpire calls 'No-ball!' if the bowler puts a foot over the back or side lines of the square during the bowling action. Since bowlers' actions differ, the umpire must move about to keep a clear view of the moment the ball is released.

- When the ball goes dead, it is the bowler's umpire who indicates this by calling 'Dead'.

 The bowler's umpire in position.

UMPIRE'S TEST

Details of the umpire's test can be obtained from the NRA Umpire's Secretary at the website given on page 56.

VARIATIONS

Rounders is a game that is accessible to all people, including those with special needs and disabilities. The game can be adapted to meet the needs of everyone's ability. When adapting rounders, it is important to adhere to the spirit of the game.

T-BALL ROUNDERS

This version of rounders is ideal for younger players who are developing hand-eye coordination.

- Minimum number of players: four per team.

- Batting team: four batters.

- Fielding team: three deep fielders; one player to cover the posts and put the ball on the T-stand.

- Equipment: one T-stand or large cone; one suitable ball; four bats (one for each player); four cones as posts.

The rules are the same as standard NRA rules, except for the following:

1. The ball is placed on the T-stand for the batter to hit.

2. The batter scores one point for reaching first post (before the ball is called dead), two points for second, three points for third, six points for a rounder.

3. A team is out when batters have been put out four times, but when individuals are out they can rejoin the waiting line and they can bat again and be out again.

4. The dead-ball rule: batters can continue to run until the ball is dead. The ball is dead from when the post ahead of the 'live' batter is touched until the next batter hits the ball off the T-stand.

Adaptation

T-ball rounders can be used and adapted for all those who have difficulty in hitting a moving ball. Rule changes may need to be made to suit the ability of the group or individuals. Whatever the changes, though, the name of the game is still rounders!

Other variations can be found in the NRA publication Rounders Practices. Details of all NRA publications can be obtained from the NRA Publications Secretary at the website on page 56.

EQUIPMENT CHANGES

These are suggested adaptations or changes to the equipment used for rounders, depending on the abilities of the players:

- use larger/smaller balls – foam, air flow, ball with 'bell', bean-bag ball, etc.
- use lower or lighter equipment – cones, plastic bats, padder bats, paddlebats, etc.
- use brightly coloured equipment
- use batting Ts, e.g. a cone with a ball on the top, for those who have difficulty hitting moving balls
- reduce the playing area, e.g. use three posts instead of four.

Always use a variety of equipment to engage younger players and to build success.

Batters can be stumped out in all versions of rounders.

THE NRA

The governing body for rounders is the National Rounders Association (NRA) which was formed in 1943. The NRA is responsible for the rules and development of the game worldwide.

'MAKING A DIFFERENCE'

Rounders is supported financially by Sport England as a priority development sport, and has a four-year development plan called 'Making a Difference'.

The NRA wants to develop more coaches and officials, and increase its structure of paid staff and volunteers. This will help it to serve the needs of member leagues and schools, which will then be able to participate in the many sporting opportunities that are available today.

COACHING AND UMPIRING COURSES

A programme of coaching and umpiring courses, and a range of resources, are available to support the sport. These include the Basic Skills Award. Competitions are organised annually, at regional and international levels.

The NRA aims to help players develop from playground to podium, and provide the support for them to achieve at whatever level they desire. You can help them do this by joining the NRA.

Even national umpire tutors consult before making an important decision.

Membership also means you will keep up to date with what is happening in rounders, as well as receiving support in developing the sport in your area. Contact the NRA at the following:

www.nra-rounders.co.uk
National Office tel 0114 2480357
Email nra.office@btopenworld.com

TOURNAMENTS

Details of NRA tournaments are available from the NRA Tournament Secretary at the website given above.

AWARDS SCHEME

Details of the NRA Awards Scheme are available from the NRA Schools Secretary at the website given above.

 In or out? Tournaments often include competitive games.

GLOSSARY

Backstop Fielder who stands behind the batting square to field the ball.

Backward hit When the ball is hit into the backward area. Batters can only run to first post. Once the ball is thrown by a fielder and crosses the forward/backward line they can run on.

Ball Should be made of leather, weigh between 65 and 85g, and measure between 18 and 20cm in circumference.

Ball in play The ball is in play from the time it leaves the bowler's hand until he or she again has possession of the ball and is in the square.

Bat Can be of any length up to a maximum of 46cm. It should not be more than 17cm round the thickest part or weigh more than 370g. Bats are made of wood, aluminium or plastic.

Batter Stands in the batting square to hit the ball.

Batting square 2m x 2m area where the batter stands to receive the ball.

Bowler Player on the fielding team who throws the ball to the batter.

Bowling square 2.5m x 2.5m area where the bowler stands to bowl the ball.

Captain Takes responsibility for the team and makes fielding and batting decisions.

Changing the field When the captain moves fielders to anticipate where the batter is likely to hit, for instance for strong or weak players, or for left-handers.

Deep fielders Players who field away from the posts, towards the edges of the playing area.

Donkey-drop A high ball that falls downwards to reach the batter at the correct height.

First-post fielder A fielder who stands at first post, working closely with the backstop to get batters out.

Fourth-post fielder A fielder placed on the fourth post.

Half-rounder Scored if, after hitting the ball, the batter reaches second post and is not out before another ball is bowled OR after missing the ball, the batter runs round the track and touches the fourth post OR if the fielder, in the opinion of the umpire, obstructs the batter OR is awarded to the opposing team if a batter, while waiting to bat, obstructs a fielder.

Innings A full game consists of two innings per team; the team with the greater number of rounders wins. An innings is over when there are no members of the batting team available to bat.

Mixed teams Teams with males and females in them; mixed teams can have a maximum of five males.

NRA The National Rounders Association, the governing body of rounders.

Obstruction When the batter impedes any fielder, when running or batting; or when a fielder impedes a batter.

Overarm throw When the ball is thrown above or about the level of the shoulders.

Pitch The playing area. Can be any surface on which it is possible to run quickly (e.g. asphalt, all weather or grass), though mixed surfaces are not recommended. The area needed is about the size of a soccer pitch.

Posts Four posts are used, each 1.2m high

Rounder Score made when the batter hits the ball and then runs round four posts.

Second-post fielder Fielder who stands at second post to field. Also partly a deep fielder.

Side out When a whole team is put out in one go.

Stay The batter may 'stay', or stop, at any post on the way round.

Substitutes Replacement players. Any or all of six substitutes, named before the start of the game, can join in at any dead-ball situation.

T-ball rounders Alternative form of rounders, where the ball is placed on a T-stand or large cone for the batter to hit.

Third-post fielder Fielder on the third post. Frequently receives catches and many low-driven ground balls.

Underarm throwing When the ball is thrown from below the level of the shoulders.

ROUNDERS CHRONOLOGY

1744 The game of rounders has been played in England since Tudor times, with the earliest reference being in 1744, in *A Little Pretty Pocketbook,* where it is called 'baseball'. This explains why the two games are similar, and in fact many students of baseball accept that their sport is derived from rounders. The name 'rounders' was used by Jane Austen in *Northanger Abbey* (1817).

1828 *The Boy's Own Book* of 1828 devotes a chapter to rounders.

1889 The Liverpool and Scottish Rounders Association is formed. The first official rules remove the practice of putting a running batter out by hitting them with a thrown ball.

1892 Rounders rule book published, containing the oldest set of rules the National Rounders Association are aware of.

1943 The Women's Team Games Board form a National Rounders Association. It is responsible for the rules of the game and for arranging national tests for umpires and coaches. Rounders remains mainly a game for schoolchildren, but played by adults on the beach or in parks.

1968 The Sheffield Works Sports Association affiliates to the NRA. The association was formed in 1919, and a Rounders section had been started in 1961.

1976 Rhyl host the first National Tournament. Much to their surprise they find the greatest demand for entries comes from the mixed adult clubs. Sheffield Club wins the first tournament.

1977 Rhyl and Sheffield organise the first Representative match between England and Wales. Matches are now played at Senior and Under 21 levels on a home and away basis.

1982 The England Squad visits the USA to introduce the game of rounders to softball teams in Florida. Predictably, the Americans win at softball and the English win at rounders.

1984 Leicestershire is the first county to form a County Association for rounders.

1988 When Dublin celebrates its millennium in 1988, England teams are invited to take part in some matches against Irish rounders teams. The Irish game is very similar to softball. A mixed Irish team has since visited England to take part in the National Tournaments.

2001 The England Under-18 team travels to Toronto, Canada to introduce rounders to softball clubs there.

2005 The England Senior team competes in the Gary Kelly Cup in Ireland, and junior teams tour the Isle of Man and the Channel Islands.

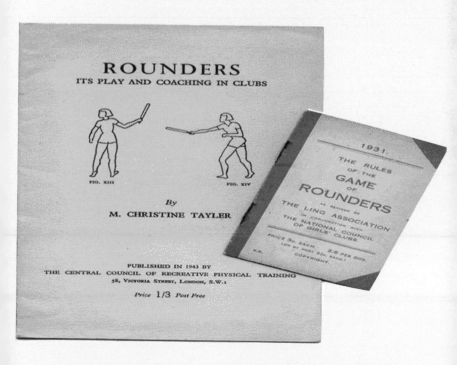

ROUNDERS
ITS PLAY AND COACHING IN CLUBS

FIG. XIII

FIG. XIV

By
M. CHRISTINE TAYLER

PUBLISHED IN 1943 BY
THE CENTRAL COUNCIL OF RECREATIVE PHYSICAL TRAINING
58, Victoria Street, London, S.W.1

Price 1/3 Post Free

1931.

THE RULES
OF THE
GAME
OF
ROUNDERS
AS REVISED BY
THE LING ASSOCIATION
IN CONJUNCTION WITH
THE NATIONAL COUNCIL
OF GIRLS' CLUBS

PRICE 3D. EACH. 2/6 PER DOZ.
(OR BY POST 3½D. EACH)
COPYRIGHT.

INDEX